S0-DOQ-456

The HAPPY Birthday Book

THE HAPPY BIRTHDAY BOOK

By Benjamin Whitley
Illustrated by Marilyn Conklin

Hallmark Editions

Copyright © 1972 by Hallmark Cards, Inc.,
Kansas City, Missouri. All Rights Reserved.
Printed in the United States of America.
Library of Congress Catalog Card Number: 72-187537.
Standard Book Number: 87529-260-7.

The HAPPY Birthday Book

A birthday is
a HAPPY time—
It's your personal holiday
For doing the things
you like to do...

And for doing things
YOUR way.

It's a time for SMILES
and LAUGHTER,
A day for having fun
From the first gold rays
of morning...

Until the day is done.

A birthday
is an EXCITING time,
With new joys
to pursue...

The world's a big,
wide and beautiful place,
And today
it belongs to you!

It is a time for "living high,"
So set your "fancy" free --
Get ready, get set
and let yourself go...

You're the DAY'S celebrity!

A birthday is a time
to DREAM
Of all the special things
The year ahead
may hold in store,
The pleasures it will bring.

It's a time to spend
RECALLING
The joys
the year has brought...

A day for visiting
with friends—
In person...or in thought.

A birthday
is a CAREFREE time,
A day that's
bright and breezy...

When you should
put your work away,
Relax and take it easy!

It's a time
to have a PARTY,
A very special date...

And no matter
how you do it,
It's a day to celebrate!

A birthday
is for WISHING,
And yours will come about
If you will wish
with all your might...

Then blow the candles out.

It's a time for CARDS
and PRESENTS,
And every special minute
Will bring a nice surprise
for you...

With birthday magic in it.

The day is really
WONDERFUL—
A time to sing and play...

For it's the anniversary
Of your very own
BIRTH day!

HAPPY BIRTHDAY!

write me soon,

Carol Smith